Wonders of His Grace
Greg Albrecht

G**race is a multi-layered word.** Its many definitions add rich perspectives and significance to our lives. Grace speaks of abundance and gratitude, of charm and inner beauty, of harmony, mercy and forgiveness. We say grace before a meal. A dancer or figure skater is graceful. When a debt is owed and a bill is due, grace periods are offered before penalties begin. The world of music speaks of grace notes.

Within the faith community, the standard definition of God's grace is "the unmerited favor of God." That definition is a good start—it is worth mulling over day by day—but it does not completely capture God's boundless and eternal grace. The many facets of this multi-layered word reveal how God imparts his favor to ALL of us who, no matter our efforts or lack thereof, deserve nothing from him. It is a gift, not a paycheck. Grace cannot be earned, only given. God's grace can be rejected and it can be embraced.

When we receive God's grace, we yield our trifling and futile attempts to impress him and willingly surrender our ways to his, so that his love and mercy may have its way with us. Embracing God's grace means surrendering any and all pretexts we have of earning his favor so that we might, without reservation, trust and rest in him.

When we receive God's grace, we turn our backs on spiritual and religious darkness and begin walking toward the Light of Christ. When we receive God's grace, we are transformed into the divine dimension where God's love reigns supreme such that he graciously imparts spiritual vision that enables us to perceive, little by little, the *Wonders of His Grace*.

Grace flows downward from divinity to humanity. God's grace descends from immortality to mortality, from perfection to imperfection. God's grace is somewhat like water that inevitably finds and is welcomed in low places. Conversely, grace finds resistance in religious high places.

God gives grace to the humble, but he resists the proud and haughty as they sit astride their spiritual high horses. The spiritually proud see God's grace as unnecessary and even as a sign of weakness, like a crutch, so grace cascades off their souls like the proverbial water "off a duck's back."

Grace is like streams and rivers filled and nourished by the rain. Life-giving rain is given to those whose lives seem to deserve it and to those who do not (Matthew 5:45). The rain (and reign) of God's grace resists attempts to collect, own and dispense it by those who live in high places of religious pride and announce themselves as God's representatives.

The prophet Isaiah reveals God inviting those who thirst to "come to the waters"– inviting those who *"have no money, 'Come, buy and eat!'"* (Isaiah 55:1). Jesus invited those who are thirsty, *"Come to me and drink"*—he assures us that *"rivers of living water"* will flow from within those who believe in him (John 7:37-38).*"The river of the water of life, as clear as crystal"* will flow from the throne of God in the new Jerusalem, come down from heaven as a part of a new heaven and new earth (Revelation 22:1).

As Christ-followers, we are invited to be immersed and swim in the river of God's grace which fills our every need. God's grace cleanses, sustains and empowers us so that we enjoy and rejoice in the pure love and mercy of God rather than the swamps and cesspools of corruption all around us. As his children, God's grace redeems and saves us from our liabilities that religion insists we must reconcile to earn God's love. God's grace delivers us from cynicism, doubt and fear—it lifts us out of the hateful day-to-day reality that is part of living in our world—giving us eyes to see above and beyond our hurts and depression.

We cannot achieve or acquire God's grace. Grace is not an achievement any more than we can look at the beauty of his creation and

Wonders of His Grace

Copyright © 2020
CWR Press
Greg Albrecht

Photos by Ron Kelly

Scriptures cited from
The Message© by Eugene Peterson

ISBN: 978-1-889973-36-4

Printed in Canada

Graphic Design: Brad Jersak

Pasadena, CA | www.ptm.org

claim credit for designing and creating it. God's grace is not a thing—it cannot be purchased by good deeds. We do not "have" or "own" or "possess" God's grace. Rather, we float in the river of God's grace. God's grace suspends and surrounds us.

God's grace is a wonder–a miracle! God's grace is a gift that allows Christ followers to see God and his magnificent creation with child-like awe.

If you live in a big city, take time for a drive out beyond the city lights, pull over where it is safe, get out of your car and look up. When our gaze is locked onto our horizontal lives, we limit our spiritual perspectives to the tunnel vision of our horizontal reality. We're distracted by busyness and fail to perceive, marvel and be astounded by God's wonders.

Look up into the sky at the vast panorama of stars. The stars of God are unlike city lights powered by electricity with bulbs that must be replaced. The constellations and galaxies created by God keep shining as they have for billions of years.

Go to the beach or shore and consider the power and majesty of the ocean. Watch those mighty breakers crash down upon the sand and rocks, and marvel that they have been relentlessly arriving at the edge of the ocean before you and I were residing on this earth, and they will continue to after we have long gone.

Go outside when it rains, and allow the rain to cascade down on you. Look up and open your mouth that your thirst might be quenched from above.

The *Wonders of His Grace* enable us to look up and beyond daily life, with all of its cares and worries–his grace lifts us beyond the pain and desperation of humanity into his eternal joy so that we might bask in who God is and how he reveals himself to us through his creation.

The secret of God's grace is that we must stop trying to make God love us and surrender to let him love us on his terms. When we surrender our works and give way to God's work, he shines his wondrous grace and illuminating light within us, so that we as his children may reflect his wonders and his grace.

Grace is the amazing wonder of God–it is counter-intuitive because it is often not given in ways we think fair, appropriate and just. We like to see people get what's coming to them. God loves to forgive. We prefer to earn our own way–God insists that our salvation is nothing we have earned. It is a *Wonder of his Grace.*

According to religious expectations and definitions, many of the parables of Jesus make the wrong person the hero. Who stars in the parables of Jesus? Who shines? The wasteful prodigal son, not the obedient elder brother–the good Samaritan (despised by religion) rather than Jewish rabbis (admired and honored by religion)–the scorned and reviled tax collector who did not even look up to heaven as he prayed rather than the righteous Pharisee—the poor, homeless beggar named Lazarus and not the rich man.

Grace is like water and rain, but is it also like the wind. We have no idea where wind comes from but there is no doubt that wind is also a metaphor of God's grace.

"The wind blows wherever it pleases. You hear its sound, but you cannot tell where it comes from or where it is going. So it is with everyone who is born of the Spirit" (John 3:8).

If an event or experience doesn't predictably run down the roads of righteousness constructed by religion, then it is often dismissed as trivial or irrelevant. If something happens that doesn't fit with religious expectations, many people discount or disregard the incident. If something is not planned, organized or structured in such a way people have been religiously indoctrinated to think of as correct and appropriate, they are tempted to minimize, belittle or even deprecate it. Some say of things that don't fit the box they have God in—"it can't be God's plan for my life."

But God's grace is like the wind. One can hear, feel and see the effects of wind without completely understanding how wind works and where it comes from. The grace of God is like pollen carried by the wind, spreading life. The grace of God is like the wind filling our sails.

God's grace is liberation from religious propaganda and authoritarian, tyrannical indoctrination. God's grace is deliverance from superstition, fear, shame and guilt. God's grace is emancipation from spiritual slavery and bondage.

The following photographs and biblical passages have been selected so that we might marvel at the *Wonders of His Grace.* Toward this end, I am thankful that Ron Kelly, my friend of many decades, has allowed us to publish some of his remarkable photographs. I am thankful for the graphic design of these pages, contributed by my friend and colleague, Brad Jersak. Join me in reflecting, pondering and wondering—in giving thanks and with gratitude—for the *Wonders of His Grace.*

—Greg Albrecht, President of PTM

The Word was first,
the Word present to God,
God present to the Word.
The Word was God,
in readiness for God from day one.
Everything was created through him;
nothing—not one thing!—
came into being without him.
What came into existence was Life,
and the Life was Light to live by.
The Life-Light
blazed out of the darkness;
the darkness couldn't put it out.
John 1:1-5

God is sheer mercy
and grace;

not easily angered,
he's rich in love . . .

As high as heaven
is over the earth,
so strong is his love
to those who fear him.

And as far as sunrise
is from sunset,
he has separated us
from our sins.

Psalm 103:7,9

Take a good look at God's wonders—
they'll take your breath away.
He converted sea to dry land;
travelers crossed the river on foot.
Now isn't that cause for a song?

Psalm 66:5-6

You did it:
you changed wild lament
into whirling dance;
You ripped off my black mourning band
and decked me with wildflowers.
I'm about to burst with song;
I can't keep quiet about you.
God, my God, I can't thank you enough.

Psalm 30:11-12

Who has scooped up the ocean
in his two hands,
or measured the sky between his
thumb and little finger,
Who has put all the earth's dirt in
one of his baskets,
weighed each mountain and hill?

Isaiah 40:12-13

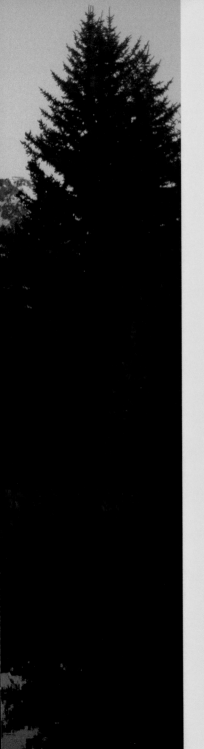

How beautiful on the mountains are the feet of the messenger bringing good news,

Breaking the news that all's well, proclaiming good times, announcing salvation, telling Zion, "Your God reigns!"

Isaiah 52:7

We look at this Son and see the God who cannot be seen. We look at this Son and see God's original purpose in everything created.

For everything, absolutely everything, above and below, visible and invisible, rank after rank after rank of angels—*everything* got started in him and finds its purpose in him.

He was there before any of it came into existence and holds it all together right up to this moment. And when it comes to the church, he organizes and holds it together, like a head does a body.

He was supreme in the beginning and—leading the resurrection parade—he is supreme in the end. From beginning to end he's there, towering far above everything, everyone.

So spacious is he, so roomy, that everything of God finds its proper place in him without crowding.

Not only that, but all the broken and dislocated pieces of the universe—people and things, animals and atoms—get properly fixed and fit together in vibrant harmonies, all because of his death, his blood that poured down from the Cross.

Colossians 1:15-20

Listen, Heavens,
  I have something to tell you.
Attention, Earth,
  I've got a mouth full of words.
My teaching,
  let it fall like a gentle rain,
  my words arrive like morning dew,
Like a sprinkling rain on new grass,
  like spring showers on the garden.
For it's God's Name I'm preaching—
  respond to the greatness of our God!

The Rock:
His works are perfect,
  and the way he works is fair and just;
A God you can depend upon,
  no exceptions,
  a straight-arrow God.
Deuteronomy 32:1-4

You're my cave to hide in, my cliff to climb.
Be my safe leader, be my true mountain guide.
Free me from hidden traps; I want to hide in you.
I've put my life in your hands.
You won't drop me, you'll never let me down.

Psalm 31:3-5

"...walk out into the fields and look at the wild-flowers. They never primp or shop, but have you ever seen color and design quite like it?... If God gives such attention to the appearance of wild-flowers—most of which are never even seen—don't you think he'll attend to you, take pride in you, do his best for you?"

Matthew 6:28, 30

Hey there!
All who are thirsty, come to the water!
Are you penniless?
Come anyway—buy and eat!
Come, buy your drinks, buy wine and milk.
Buy without money—everything's free!

Isaiah 55:1-2

Who do you suppose carves canyons
for the downpours of rain, and charts
the route of thunderstorms
That bring water to unvisited fields,
deserts no one ever lays eyes on,
Drenching the useless wastelands
so they're carpeted
with wildflowers and grass?

Job 38:25-27

As the earth bursts with spring wildflowers,
and as a garden cascades with blossoms,
So the Master, GOD,
brings righteousness into full bloom
and puts praise on display
before the nations.

Isaiah 61:11

How well God must like you—
　you don't hang out at Sin Saloon,
　you don't slink along Dead-End Road,
　you don't go to Smart-Mouth College.

Instead you thrill to God's Word,
　you chew on Scripture day and night.

You're a tree replanted in Eden,
　bearing fresh fruit every month,
Never dropping a leaf,
　always in blossom.

Psalm 1:1-3

O my soul, bless God!
God, my God, how great you are!
  beautifully, gloriously robed,
Dressed up in sunshine,
  and all heaven stretched out for your tent.

You blanketed earth with ocean,
  covered the mountains with deep waters;
Then you roared and the water ran away—
  your thunder crash put it to flight.

Mountains pushed up,
  valleys spread out in the places
  you assigned them.
You set boundaries between earth and sea;
  never again will earth be flooded.

You started the springs and rivers,
  sent them flowing among the hills.
All the wild animals now drink their fill,
  wild donkeys quench their thirst.

Along the riverbanks the birds build nests,
  ravens make their voices heard.
You water the mountains
  from your heavenly cisterns;
  earth is supplied with plenty of water.

Psalm 104:1-2, 6-13

The God who made the world and everything in it, this Master of sky and land, doesn't live in custom-made shrines or need the human race to run errands for him, as if he couldn't take care of himself.

He makes the creatures; the creatures don't make him. Starting from scratch, he made the entire human race and made the earth hospitable, with plenty of time and space for living so we could seek after God, and not just grope around in the dark but actually find *him.*

He doesn't play hide-and-seek with us. He's not remote; he's near. We live and move in him, can't get away from him! One of your poets said it well: 'We're the God-created.' Well, if we are the God-created, it doesn't make a lot of sense to think we could hire a sculptor to chisel a god out of stone for us, does it?

Acts 17:24-29

Oh, visit the earth,
　ask her to join the dance!
Deck her out in spring showers,
　fill the God-River with living water.
Paint the wheat fields golden.
　Creation was made for this!
Drench the plowed fields,
　soak the dirt clods
With rainfall as harrow and rake
　bring her to blossom and fruit.
Snow-crown the peaks with splendor,
　scatter rose petals down your paths,
All through the wild meadows,
　rose petals. Set the hills to dancing,
Dress the canyon walls with live sheep,
　a drape of flax across the valleys.
Let them shout, and shout, and shout!
Oh, oh, let them sing!

Psalm 65:9-13

God rules.
On your toes, everybody!
He rules
  from his angel throne—
  take notice!
God looms
  majestic in Zion,
He towers in splendor
  over all the big names.
Great and terrible
  your beauty:
  let everyone praise you!
Holy. Yes, holy.
Psalm 99:1–3

God—you're my God!
I can't get enough of you!
I've worked up such hunger and thirst for God,
traveling across dry and weary deserts.

Psalm 63:1

I love you, God—
  you make me strong
God is bedrock
  under my feet,
  the castle
  in which I live,
  my rescuing knight.
My God—
  the high crag where
  I run for dear life,
  hiding behind
  boulders,
  safe in the granite
  hideout.

Psalm 18:1-2

"Are you tired? Worn out? Burned out on religion? Come to me. Get away with me and you'll recover your life. I'll show you how to take a real rest. Walk with me and work with me—watch how I do it. Learn the unforced rhythms of grace. I won't lay anything heavy or ill-fitting on you. Keep company with me and you'll learn to live freely and lightly."

Matthew 11:28-30

Photograph Descriptions